Optional Thinking

Past Realities meet Future Purposes to create Present Choices.

Donell Edmond

Copyrights © 2021 by Donell Edmond

All rights reserved. This book or any portion of thereof may not be reproduced or used in any manner whatsoever without the express written permission of the author except for the use of brief quotations in a book review.

First printing, 2021

Contents

	Page No
Preface	1
Chapter I: Reality	3
1. Accepting Your reality	7
2. Moving on	11
3. The Story	15
4. Doubt	21
Chapter II: Purpose	25
5. Defining Purpose	29
6. The Right Mindset	39
7. How Purpose Influences Your Way of Thinking	45
8. The Story Continues	47
9. Fear	51
Chapter III: Choices	55
10. Choice and Purpose	63
11. Reasoning	67
12. How to Make Choices	71
13. The Story Pursues	77
14. Worries	83
Chapter IV: Optional Thinking	87

15. The Optional Thinking Mind-set:
    Hope, Belief and Faith   99
16. The Endgame   103
17. The Story Presumes   105
18. Ways to Build Confidence
    and Overcome Worries   111
19. Who Am I?   117

Preface

This book is titled Optional Thinking and has four chapters. Each of these chapters will identify, define, and provide an alternative viewpoint of the words being discussed in them. Words such as Reality, Purpose, and Choice.

The ideal is to present to the reader an optional way of thinking, and a mind-set that recognizes the several alternatives that one could use to firstly motivate oneself, and then motivate others through the process of Optional Thinking.

My mother, Helen Frances, once said to me

"Boy, you know there is more than one way to skin a cat."

She had never skinned a cat before, but what she was trying to teach me was the idea that I always had options, and that I just had to find out how to create them for myself. I only had to open my mind to apply the illustration to whatever my reality was at that moment, and that would be the cat I needed to skin.

After figuring out the purpose for skinning the cat, it is necessary that I discover the different means and know how to complete the task. The differences that I discover are now my new choices on the step that I must take in order to achieve my set purpose, which would be to get the skin off that cat.

Oh, and to be clear, no cat was harmed or skinned in the making of this book – LOL (laughing out Loud).

It is a common belief that the choices we made in the past are what make us who we are in the future. Yesterday made us who we are today, therefore, the choices we make today massively could influence who we become tomorrow.

Having the ability to make choices gives us a great sense of awareness that we are in control of our lives. This feeling is proof that the choices we make are particularly important and that we need to be in control of our lives if we are to fulfill our life purposes. Since choice is very crucial to fulfilling our life purposes, there is a need to learn how to create choices for ourselves.

This is where Optional Thinking comes into play. In this book, we will demonstrate to you how to understand your reality, identify a life of purpose, to create new possible life choices using reasoning with self-understanding.

I

Reality

"There are some, who live in a dream world, and there are some who face reality, and then there are those who turn one into the other."

Douglas Everett

Your reality is simply what you have been through in life. This implies that your reality comprises everything you experienced in your past and the impact that those experiences have had on you. Before beginning your journey of moving on and finding purpose, there is a need to understand what your reality is. What are your physical, social and mental limits?

What are your strengths? You need to ask yourself these questions to help assess where you are right now. By doing this, you also gain insight into the things you will need to do, to get to where you want to be.

You need to know your reality. Knowing your reality is basically the first step in optional thinking. In other words, you need to know the reality about yourself and where you currently are in all aspects, before you begin to weigh the options that are available to you. When you know your limits, it becomes easier to overcome them, when you know your strengths; it becomes easier to make decisions that help you take advantage of them, as well as build on them.

Almost everyone has a past that they would prefer to forget. There is no one who has a perfect past. Everyone has that thing that they wish they could undo or erase, and there is nothing wrong with that. There are things we have done, or things that have been done to us, that we wish had not happened.

Wishing you could right the mistakes you made in the past, simply makes you a human! It makes you the same as everybody else. Thus, the desire to have the power to change the past is not unnatural!

It is quite normal to desire change or want what you do not have.

The sad truth is, as, at the time of writing this book, time travel has not been invented. There is no way to go back in time, and right the wrongs you have made. And although everyone knows this, it is possible to remain stuck with this desire to right your past for a long time and remain stagnant, living in the past. The truth is that time does not wait for anybody.

The more time you spend trying to fix your past reality, the more valuable time you lose that could be spent on making a new reality.

Everyone has a different reality. The unique experiences you had while growing up helped shape your present reality. The choices you made helped shape your present reality. Even your family, who they are and how they live, helped shape your present reality, but, irrespective of how unique your reality is, or how tough life was for you, you must realize that the past is gone and now is the best time to forge a new reality!

You must begin to think of ways to create a new reality. So maybe you were bullied a lot when you were in high school, or you constantly find yourself struggling to make ends meet. Maybe you are thirty-five and you still want to go to college, or you want to become a doctor at fifty-five. Everything is possible! If you START!

Holding on to your past is never the answer. Your reality is past! Coming to the realization that your reality is your past and realizing that NOW is the best time to forge a new reality for yourself is the mentality that you should have before you begin the art of optional thinking!

Accepting your reality and moving past it, is the only progressive reaction, and the only chance you have for a better reality in your present and future days.

1
Accepting Your Reality

"It is during our darkest moments that we must focus to see the light"

-Aristotle

The issue of accepting your reality is a very significant one and requires a lot of attention. It concerns all sorts of people, ranging from teens and young adults all the way to the elderly. It is never too late to start. Together, let us look at a few practical steps that could help you accept your reality.

1. IDENTIFY WHAT YOU DON'T LIKE ABOUT YOUR PAST

For most people who have had a terrible past, a failure to identify what exactly they do not like about their past reality is surprisingly quite common. This step of identifying what you do not like is very crucial as it helps you accept the truth about your past, and consequently it helps you move forward.

An example of this scenario is seen in fictional Tom. Tom was bullied every day at school. Over time, he began to withdraw from people. He also became very hostile towards everyone he met - these were defense mechanisms he used to keep himself safe.

Because of this, intimacy was always a struggle for him. He had brief affairs, but he never truly got close to anyone. In a bid to not be bullied, he had spent his time being hostile to everyone and pushing everyone away. In doing so, he had also missed out on good people that genuinely cared. Now forty, Tom sits on his porch and wonders where he missed it.

Tom's situation is not rare at all. As humans, we tend to change who we are in order to protect ourselves from the things that might hurt us. The trouble is that sometimes we end up growing into someone we do not want to be. The good news is, Tom can still forge a reality, and still find love, just like you can.

What Tom must do is to identify that the fear of being bullied should not hold him back and convince his mind to take the first definitive step towards becoming more receptive.

2. EMBRACE CHANGE

Another step to take when working to accept your reality is to embrace change, in your mind and in your actions. Making up your mind that you are willing to undergo the transition between your past and into your future always makes the process of coming to terms with your reality easier.

Moving on in life is an intentional change that occurs when you are ready to leave your past behind you and create a reality of your choice for yourself in the near or distant future. Like in the case of Tom in our previous example, it is necessary that Tom identifies the need to accept that he was bullied by some bad humans but not all humans are bullies. This little change in perspective will help him come to terms with who he is right now, and who he wants to be.

3. LEARN FROM OTHERS

The next step that will help you accept your reality is the willingness to learn. Over the years, many people have testified that they found it easier to accept their own realities when they read, heard about, or witnessed other people's realities.

When you meet people, who are able to accept realities that are far worse than yours and still move on to a more positive reality, you will become more motivated to come to terms with who you are and be more open-minded about the many options you still have available for yourself.

An example of this is the story of a young man who grew up with people making fun of his stuttering. He found it difficult to come to terms with this reality, and it affected other aspects of his life. He found it difficult to make new friends and to participate in activities that required him to speak to people. Deep down, he wanted to be a public speaker, but that seemed like an impossible dream.

Whenever an opportunity came to speak to people and truly make an impact, he would, as the saying goes, "call off sick" or turn down the opportunity to speak.

This was his go-to response until he finally attended a seminar where the key speaker was a professor who stuttered. This professor received a resounding ovation after he was done speaking. Witnessing this made the young man realize that by not accepting the reality of his stuttering, he was preventing himself from becoming who he wanted to be. He realized he been running from his true self and had not been willing to change to make his new reality possible.

2
Moving On

"The greatest glory in living lies not in never falling but rising every time"

Nelson Mandela

You might ask yourself, *"Why should I excitedly try to forge a new reality, especially when the future is not certain to be a better one?"*

Firstly, it is important that you realize that if you do not actually try, you might never know how very different, how much better your life can be. Moving on, whether it is a toxic relationship, a job that is holding your back, the loss of a loved one, or anything of the sort, has a very positive effect on your life. The ability to bring this positivity is in your hands alone. You hold the ability to find out the truth for yourself. Understand your reality to keep moving forward and move on. There is something liberating about moving on from a past reality.

It is true that these situations are bad for anyone, but you need to realize that moving on from them will bring an aura of positivity that you will need for building your courage and your confidence. A popular quote by Wayne Misner sums it all up.

"Keeping baggage from the past will leave no room for happiness in the future".

A good example of this is the story of the young man who accepted his reality of stuttering in the previous chapter. Accepting this reality and deciding to move on gave him a positive mentality and newfound strength that allowed him to see his options.

There simply is no time left to waste! There is absolutely no time to wallow in negative feelings! And that is what you would be doing by holding on to your negative past! Holding on results in your letting precious and irredeemable time in your life go to waste.

Kevin Hart, an American producer, stand-up comedian, and actor, was raised in a family that does not necessarily classify as an ideal definition of a happy home. According to him, his father did terrible things to him.

His father threw him into a pool knowing full well his son could not swim. He angrily brought Kevin to the wrong camp and left him there, he ruined Kevin's spelling bee. The list goes on interminably.

According to Kevin, he never saw the happy years between his parents. His mother was the only encouragement he had because of the strength she showed and the financial and emotional support she always gave him.

For him, this reality is the reason he made up his mind to be a good father to his children and to be a good example of what a father should be like. He wanted a different reality for his children! In his words, he said,

> "I know what it's like not to be a good dad. I learned that because of mistakes that my dad made and because of that, I burst my ass to get back home to see my kids. I can tell my dad is the way he is for a reason. You are a product of your environment. Today, I know that nothing beats the relationship that you have with your kids".
>
> - Kevin Hart

Like Kevin Hart, you do not just reel in the bad experiences you had while growing up! You get up and create a new reality for yourself! Rather than being crushed by your past, you find strength.

You can make the choice to come out of experiences like these stronger and more determined to make a better life for yourself. This puts you in a position to have a positive impact on the people around you. You deserve a bright future, letting go of your dark past is the best choice you will ever make.

Many people allow their past to be the entire story of who they are. They accept that past reality as the story of their lives and live accordingly. This mentality is the reason many people are unable to move on. If you were abused in the past, it does not mean you have to be a victim now and for the rest of your life. You can begin to see yourself as a survivor instead. Understanding that you deserve more, and you can have more, is a reason for you to move on from your past.

Opportunities for a better reality only come to you when you choose to move on and act on that decision. The possibility of a better reality will not come unless you are willing to leave the past in the past and move on.

Thomas Jefferson once said

"I find that the harder I work; the more luck I seem to have"

The above quote perfectly sums up the life of everyone who accepted their reality and chose to move on. The decision to move on after a setback does not magically solve all your problems and bring you into a perfect reality, but it allows you to build on that decision to move on and consequently increases your chances of achieving a better life for yourself.

I hope that this chapter helped you realize how important it is that you accept your reality, move on and adopt the approach of always assessing your options, then picking what you believe to be the best one to move you forward to fulfill your purpose.

3

The Story

Reflecting on her past, Marie was certain there had been no happy days in the last 21 years. While people danced theatrically around her and sang at the top of their voices like crazy as the radio continued to play songs loudly, all she could think of was how they were celebrating the 21st birthday of a person who had absolutely nothing to celebrate.

Marie's mind kept drifting between different sad memories and only responded to the different compliments she was gaining from her good friends in an absent-minded way.

Marie felt that she had grown up the worst possible way anyone could ever think of. A drunk driver hit her down at twelve years old. She lost one leg in that accident. It's bad enough that she now had to live her life with one leg. But it's an uglier reality when you consider that this drunk driver was her father. On top of that, she watched her father beat up her mother every day, something that cost her mother two pregnancies. It gets worse. Many times, Marie watched her mother hopelessly get high on locally sold drugs on the couch.

Marie was almost certain that there had to be some sort of evil curse on her family. Maybe her grandparents had cursed her parents for eloping together at an incredibly young, tender age.

What other explanation could there possibly be for such never-ending unhappiness and pain?

After everyone had left her room and the party her friends threw for her was over, she drifted slowly back into her thoughts. Exactly seven years ago today, her father had just come back home after almost a month of being away as usual.

Marie had hoped that this time, her father would not return. She had hoped that something terrible, like an accident, had happened to him and that she was rid of the man who had slowly driven her mother to the brink of insanity. Her father came home drunk, as usual, and went straight to the kitchen, where he found no food in the fridge.

Her father came out cursing and screaming out his lungs about how Marie and her mother were good for nothing and had eaten all the food he claimed to always buy. Mind you, this man had not bought any food in the house since she was still a little child. Marie told her father that there had been no food in the kitchen in a long time, and that she and her mother had been barely surviving on old can goods.

Out of anger, her father threw a plate at her, but missed and hit the TV. Her father's anger escalated, and before she could bring herself to fully understand what was going on, her father pounced on her like a possessed man and started to beat on her.

Marie remembered how helpless she was on that day and did not realize that there were tears falling from her eyes. Her drunken father who, years earlier, had rendered her unable to walk without crutches was now assaulting her. Like several other assaults that followed, Marie sustained injuries all over her body, ranging from fractured ribs to a dislocated arm, swollen face, and much more.

One time, she woke up to the sound of an ambulance and wondered who needed medical attention in the building. In a few seconds, she saw her unconscious and barely clothed mother being carried out on stretchers by men in white uniforms. She did not understand what was really happening.

Who called the ambulance? What happened to my mother? All she could ever do was watch as her mother was taken away in the ambulance. Later that day, Marie's father came back home looking like a different man entirely.

She had never seen that look on her father's face before; it was as if he had just heard terrible news. She had never known her father to be sad about anything, or at least he never showed it. Her mother had died before even getting to the hospital.

Cause of death: overdose on Heroin. What Marie could never have foreseen, is the fact that her father would not be present for the mother's burial. Her dad left home the next day after her mom died and came back months after, looking exactly how he always did whenever he came back; dirty, and smelly as usual, a unique combination of the smell of garbage and alcohol.

Just last year, when she got the confirmation for her scholarship to study Journalism in college, she had another argument with her dad. She had informed her father about this scholarship and now that she thought of it, she wondered why she ever expected a sane response from him.

Her father responded by asking why she wanted to go to college and if she really thought a "one-legged" black girl could survive in such a highly competitive environment dominated by rich kids.

His exact words to Marie were "**we both know you can't make it there, so just stay here and be a loser like your daddy**". Marie in complete shock refused to let this go, out of anger she started to speak, and although she does not remember what she said to her father that day, she was sure by the expression on her father's face that he had never expected her to say them.

She has not spoken with her father since that day. "**I hope I never have to see or speak to him again**", Marie once said to a friend who came visiting.

Without the support of an only living relative that she had, Marie now had to make the decision to either resume with her colleagues to prove her father wrong or stay at home and see what other terrible things life had in store for her. A dilemma she would never wish on anyone.

We all have our various realities, some may be worse than Marie's, some may not be as bad, and like Marie, we have the decision to make on what our future reality will be. We all must make the decision of considering the options available to us in our various realities, with the knowledge that our next decision could contribute significantly to how our reality is in the near or distant future.

The ability to find a variety of options where there seems to be none, or only a few undesirable ones, is what I call Optional Thinking. As we continue to examine this concept more closely, Marie's story will shed more light on what Optional Thinking means and how it can help you improve your life.

After accepting your reality, it is necessary that you examine the options that you have. You could choose to dwell in the past, you could look for ways to improve or change your reality, you could find purpose in your current reality, and so on.

4

Doubt

Before we go to the next chapter, let's discuss something that pops into everyone's minds when the topic of moving on is mentioned, doubt. People tend to make different arguments as to why they are unable to move on. We now will look at the options they have. One common excuse people give is their inability to control everything.

They believe that there are some things that happen and there is nothing that can be done about them. This is only partially true; there are factors that are beyond our control. However, it shows signs of a lazy and pessimistic way to respond to your reality. It can be a good practice to try not to worry about the things you cannot control. It is not your role to worry about the things you cannot control, there are several other things you can control. Focus on those things. Spend your mental energies on getting those things done.

At times, this tendency to be consumed by the things over which you have no control could be a result of insecurity about different personal weaknesses. Some people are unable to move on because they think they are too old to move on, or they have gotten in too deep to move on from their current reality, or that their gender or size is not good enough for them to move on.

Do not allow yourself to be held back by your insecurities. Once you move on from them, you will discover that they were not a good enough reason to hold you back from moving on to a better reality. They will appear to be very small obstacles, whereas before they seemed to be mountains.

The thing to guard against is the feeling of hopelessness, the feeling that you have already tried everything and that nothing works, the feeling that all your efforts have been met with failure. This is where doubt can really seep into a person. I will be addressing this in the next chapter, "**Purpose**". In that chapter, we will discuss why sometimes all our efforts feel like beating a dead horse and how one could possibly escape this kind of limbo.

There is always something holding back people from moving on from their past; it may be regret, feeling defeated, disappointment from past experiences, being in denial with ourselves or even procrastination. Sometimes it's the waiting that holds us back; waiting for a better job, waiting for kids to grow up, waiting for retirement, waiting for one thing or another. This sense of doubt that comes upon us is one of the reasons so many people like you and me stay in unfulfilling situations such as the wrong job, the wrong profession, the wrong relationships, and so on.

Setting yourself free from the limitations that have imprisoned your mind is one of the best gifts you can give yourself. According to Lolly Daskal, even if you are in an unbelievably terrible situation, one of the first steps you can truly take towards improving is acknowledging it for what it is and deciding to move on. Irrespective of your reality, know it is never too late to explore the possibilities life has to offer you. It's never too late to choose the options for an opportunity to better yourself.

For now, I will leave you with this popular saying-

"The best time to plant a tree was 20 years ago! The second-best time is now!"

If you want a new reality, you might as well start today! Start now!

II
Purpose

"Your purpose in life is to find your purpose and give your whole heart and soul to it"

— Buddha

The desire to live a life of fulfillment is natural to every person. But for many reasons, not everyone gets to have their desires become a reality. One of the most common reasons for this is that people tend to make the decisions which end up with a negative outcome without identifying one's purpose, or they do not consider their options well enough before setting out on their journey for fulfillment.

This chapter will help you take a crucial step forward from accepting your reality as we discussed in the previous chapter, to getting a new focus or sense of direction in life.

In this chapter, we will talk about purpose. Your purpose should be something personal that you decide for yourself. It answers the questions; Where do you want to end up? Where do I want to be in life in the near and distant future? In the previous chapter, we discussed the idea that no matter how dismal things look, there are always multiple options available to you. You shouldn't default to the most obvious option, many times it is the option that gives you the least benefit. Remember Marie's story, the most obvious option was to resign herself to the vision (or lack thereof) that her father had for her life. She realized she deserved more. You deserve more too.

This chapter goes further to discuss why you are moving on. Without a reason for moving on, it will not be surprising if you slip back into being stuck in the past. When you decide to move on, there should be some sort of target that you have set for yourself or endgame. If your reason for moving on is to get to an endgame, what is that endgame?

Your endgame could be many things; it can be something like losing weight, getting built up, even gaining weight or any other dream that you have for yourself. This endgame is your destination and can be achieved if you set small steppingstones for yourself that are in line with that purpose.

When you make your purpose a personal feat that you aim to achieve, it helps you to build your confidence and encourages you to take meaningful steps. By setting a purpose, you feel you are more in control of your life and can be further encouraged to take the next steps because you know where you are heading. An example is that of a person going to the store to get groceries.

The store is the endgame, and this person knows that whatever actions they take now should be towards the purpose of getting to that store.

Louis Sachar once said that

"It is better to take many small steps in the right direction than to make a great leap forward only to stumble backward."

There are countless purposes for everyone that serve as steppingstones to an endgame. The knowledge that you must take one step at a time if you are to achieve your purpose gives you a sense of direction. Also, being able to accomplish these little steppingstones gives you a sense of confidence and a great feeling of achievement.

A feeling inside that you started something meaningful for yourself, you are making progress, and that you are getting closer to something that inside feels rightly meant for you, which is your purpose. The whole point of this chapter is to ask ourselves, why? Why do I want a new car, and why am I in this relationship? It should all be towards your endgame.

Asking yourself these questions will help you not only accept your past and move on, but it will also help you accept your future and embrace the possibility of fulfilling your purpose.

The greatest fear a person is faced with is the fear of the unknown. When one is confronted by a wall, there is the fear of not knowing what is beyond that wall or whether you are strong enough to go beyond that wall.

But if you make up your mind that you want to see what is on the other side of that wall, then you have set a purpose for yourself. Consequently, all your actions become channeled at going over or through that wall, rather than the fear of being hurt by that wall.

With a purpose, you become more confident to approach the unknown. With this mind-set, you become sure that to attain your purpose, you will need to cross several bridges and that you will find ways to cross those bridges when you get to each one. Problems will always come, but because of the belief and confidence your purpose brings, you have a deep feeling in you that you will overcome all problems.

5

Defining Purpose

"The greatest tragedy in life is not death, but a life without a purpose"

-Myles Munroe

According to the Oxford Dictionary, there are two main definitions for the word purpose. The first purpose **"is the reason for which something is done or created or for which something exists."**

The second definition refers to purpose as **"a person's sense of resolve or determination."** One common factor that binds both definitions together is the idea that a person or thing needs to have something that pushes them to take certain actions or make certain decisions.

Over the years, many have come up with various ideologies to help people identify their purpose or to find purpose in life. Some are of the opinion that everyone is born with a specific special purpose that has been programmed into them, or that your purpose in life is tied to the talents you have naturally. The common analogy used here is that of an invention.

The analogy states that everything that is created was made with intent; a screwdriver's purpose is to screw nails, a knife's purpose is to cut things, a pen's only purpose is to write. Using any of these things for any other function, according to this view, will be against its purpose.

Some have a rather more objective approach to purpose and how to find a purpose for yourself. They define purpose as that plan you have for yourself and hope to accomplish at a point in your life. This means that your purpose should be determined by you alone. In the previous chapter, we looked at the story of Marie and the loss and pain she suffered growing up.

Marie found herself in a situation where she had to come to terms with her past negative reality and decide how to move towards her future reality. Just like her, we all have little or no role to play in deciding the kind of reality we are born into, and like her also, we all must realize that it is our obligation to think critically and consider our options in the attempt to move on from our past reality to forge a new reality.

It is quite reasonable to predict that the person who lives their life without purpose, will likely feel unfulfilled at the end of their lives. You may decide that you want to live a life of abundance, but without the will to even try or that resolve, it is practically impossible to achieve this steppingstone. It is your purpose that will fuel you during your journey; it keeps you going no matter what obstacles life throws at you. That purpose, no matter how long it takes to embrace it, now influences the choices you make. It boosts up your courage and confidence in the face of adversity.

You can imagine how much pressure Marie, in our previous chapter, was feeling and how much she wanted to quit and give in to her past. Losing a leg, losing her mother to a premature and tragic end, and all the while having a drunk and violent father as her only living relative, is more adversity than most of us will ever have to bear.

But as you will see later in this chapter, Marie did not quit, she chose to pursue her dream and choose the options that were in line with the purpose she chose for herself.

"All our dreams can come true if we have the courage to pursue them".

- Walt Disney

As a person, what is the purpose that drives you? For many, the reason they are not able to move on from their reality is that they find themselves believing there is no light at the end of the proverbial tunnel. In fact, sometimes it is necessary to keep pushing forward in blind faith, with your purpose in mind, even when there seems to be no evidence that things will get better. When one has a purpose, it spurs you to look within and outside yourself for ways to change or improve your current reality.

The moment when you decide you will live life with a purpose or to get your endgame, is when your possible journey truly begins.

Accepting your own reality is a monumental step forward, and making the decision to bring out positivity for yourself in the difficult reality is another big step in the right direction. The next question you need to answer is **"Why?"** Why am I trying to lose weight? Why am I taking this course? Why am I making these investments? Why am I starting this business or company? Why am I going in this direction?

You need to take time out to ask yourself why you are taking these steps. If the reason for your decisions or actions is not in line with your purpose, then there is a good possibility that you will fail. It is the answer to the many questions that you have asked yourself that will help you consider your options and draft a road map for yourself.

This roadmap includes the steps you have chosen to take, the small options available to you that you chose, and the plans that you have set up in order to achieve that endgame.

The truth is, when you find your purpose, it is never certain that the steps you take will certainly lead to the fulfillment of your purpose. There are several factors that could influence the possibility of living a fulfilled life. There are limitations in the form of social factors, natural occurrences, human contribution and so on.

But there is a good possibility that weighing your options and picking the most rational option that supports your purpose will play a huge and significant role in propelling you towards a fulfilled life.

Through optional thinking, you find options for yourself that serve as stepping stones to your purpose. When you know who you are, what your strengths and limitations are, then you can decide where you want to end up. That is, you know your starting point, and you know your destination.

One of the reasons for failed stepping stones is isolation or a product of isolation. On the journey to fulfilling a purpose, it is necessary that you identify people who have the same goals as you or have a similar purpose as you do.

Ever heard the phrases knowledge is power and information is key? This applies in all areas of life, and purpose is one of those areas. If you know what you want and why you want it, then you will be confident about getting that thing. Knowledge strengthens your faith.

The world is a large place and has a lot of opportunities in it. Sometimes these opportunities are hiding in plain sight. Without the right lenses, they can go unnoticed our whole lives. Reading can shift our thinking and give us a new lens, with which to view the world around us.

Reading allows us to connect with people in various parts of the world and even in different lifetimes. It allows us to experience the things they experienced without having to be there when they happened. Learning about certain people and their experiences brings meaning to certain things, and with meaning comes purpose.

For example, various studies have proven that people who study the bible tend to have a similar reason for why they exist and the things that they must do in this world to be fulfilled. This similarity is a result of the fact that for them, they have been exposed to the similar experiences of biblical truths and this influences how they see life as a whole and their role in it.

By seeing purpose in the lives of the people they read about, people are more likely to see it in their own lives too. In this sense, reading has influenced their imagination and allowed them to find a purpose for themselves. Various great people have attested to the fact that their view of life and their role in it changed when they have read certain books.

Ronald Reagan was heavily influenced by Whittaker Chambers' book, *Witness*.

This great book narrates the experience of Chambers in the trial of Alger Hiss, a man who was accused of Soviet espionage, but never convicted. According to Reagan, the book mainly helped him to understand the way a typical communist, thinks and consequently fueled his optimism in the dream for a more conservative world.

America's first African American President, Barack Obama says that Joseph Conrad's *Heart of*

Darkness taught him empathy. He credits the book with his understanding of whites who had only negative ideas about blacks. According to him, the book helped him grasp the fears and psychological events that make people "**learn to hate**" each other.

Lastly, Donald Trump, a former President, and billionaire who made his fortune in real estate developments, says he could not have achieved all that he achieved without Dr. Normal Vincent Peale's book *The Power of Positive Thinking*.

In this self-help book, the author tells his readers to "**stand up to an obstacle**" and that by doing this, "**it will finally break**." He goes on to tell his readers that if they want to be successful, they should "**formulate and stamp indelibly on your mind a mental picture of yourself as succeeding.**" Books can open your eyes, show you opportunities, change your life; but first, you must read them.

So, if you want to find your purpose, one way of identifying and gaining information about what could be a possible steppingstone towards your endgame is to go to the bookstore, local library, nowadays you can even try finding eBook's online that matter to you. Books can also deliver realities that can help you find steppingstones that will help you focus and give you a good sense of direction.

Furthermore, reading gives you awareness of numerous options that are available to choose from, and more importantly, they showcase examples of people who have applied optional thinking (finding a variety of options, where there seems to be only a few bad ones) and reaped remarkable results.

With the insights you gain from reading, you are better equipped to survey your options. Steppingstones begin to materialize; you begin to have a better sense of direction. Your purpose shines through with clarity.

Another key step in considering your options is helping others. Just as we need the information to help us, we all need a good level of emotional maturity to be a success. Many people have chosen to dedicate their lives to impacting the lives of other people because of the emotional connection that they have with them or the situation that they are in.

Some have made up their minds to achieve certain steppingstones, especially financial ones, because of their desire to improve the lives of loved ones, or even strangers who are financially crippled. There are people who have chosen to go into the medical field because they want to contribute to the building of a world where people who cannot afford care have access to the best available medical services as those who can.

In most cases, these emotional connections are a result of some experience that they had in the past. These emotional experiences are usually the kind that impacts their lives in a hugely significant way. They draw their purpose in helping people who have been similarly affected, or in righting or wrong, or in ensuring that something like that never happens again.

Kevin Hart was raised in a family that does not necessarily classify as an ideal definition of a happy home. But people in similar situations like Kevin Hart find purpose even in some of the worst experiences they had been through even as a child growing up, rather than being crushed by them.

These emotional situations and experiences make them stronger and give them the motivation to want to be better for themselves and for the people around them. However, you do not have to wait until you have a terrible experience before finding your purpose.

You can draw motivation from the things happening all around you. You can also build on your positive reality to motivate yourself to reinvent a purpose that will ultimately lead you to your new reality.

6
The Right Mind-set

After making up a decision on what your life's purpose is, it is only ideal that you have the right mental approach towards your purpose. As you strive to achieve these steppingstones that will help you achieve your purpose, there are three key things you should keep in mind in order to stay on track.

1. FOCUS

> **"Lack of direction, not lack of time, is the problem. We all have twenty-four-hour days."**
>
> **-Zig Ziglar**

If you are going to achieve your steppingstones, it is necessary that you are constantly aware of all the reasons for every action that you take.

It is not uncommon that people lose sight of why they started their journey in the first place, and because of this loss of focus, they also lose their direction. It is easy to get distracted by so many things, especially pleasurable things, but it requires a high level of discipline in a person to live a fulfilled life.

Losing focus is a major reason why many make mistakes when deciding about something important or when taking an action. Rather than weigh all the options available to them, they are distracted and make hasty decisions that produce negative outcomes, and as expected, there are always consequences. A person who is driven by purpose needs to always stay focused if their intention is to make progress.

In the journey to success, there are always so many obstacles, distractions and setbacks. One of the key principles you will need to overcome these hindrances is staying focused.

2. SERENITY

"Serenity is knowing that your worst shot is still pretty good"

-Johnny Miller

There is nothing wrong with being concerned about the options available to you or what the results of each option will be if you take them. However, it is necessary that you always maintain a level head and try to be in a peaceful, untroubled mind-set, especially when making those decisions.

Over time, researchers have proven that being calm and in control of your emotions when making decisions based on evidence, reduces one's chances of making mistakes and helps one to notice errors quickly before they have a big impact. Consciously take one step at a time; it is alright not to move too fast.

In fact, moving at your own pace is the best way to quickly achieve your laid down goals. Decide to put your eggs in different baskets, this way you have various things to fall back on and ensure that you are never caught unawares by the inevitable bumps on the way.

Another reason for you to embrace serenity when considering options that are related to your purpose, is that it allows you to enjoy the process of decision-making. Although it is possible to claim that worrying may have a few advantages of its own, very few professionals will recommend it.

3. PURSUIT

"It's better to die in pursuit of your dreams than to live a life without hope."

-Terry Brooks

Pursuit refers to the action of pursuing someone or something. This definition implies that there is a goal or destination in mind.

As a person who is driven by purpose, there are goals you must attain in order to get closer to achieving that purpose. For example, for a person who believes that his or her purpose is to become a bodybuilder or a fitness trainer, there are several options available to such a person. You could decide to visit the gym or work out from home, you could decide to have a diet or eat as you like, and you could decide to take several things into consideration.

However, it is highly advisable that you only consider the options that will help you fulfill your purpose. A person with a purpose to fulfill should always have the mind-set that he or she is in pursuit and there are always decisions to be made at different stages of this pursuit.

A good example of a man who had the right mind-set is a man who is regarded by many as the greatest basketball player in the history of the sport, Michael Jordan. When Michael Jordan first tried out for his high school basketball team, he did not make varsity. In one of his interviews, he said

"It was embarrassing not making that team. They posted the roster, and it was there for a long, long time without my name on it. I remember being really mad too because there was a guy that made it that really wasn't as good as me."

-Michael Jordan

Michael Jordan, because of his deep desire to create a reality for himself, which was a future in which he saw himself as a professional basketball player, did not let this setback stop him from being focused, instead, during practice he was calm and channeled this embarrassment into motivation. His pursuit made him take steps that only brought him closer to his purpose. He said:

> **"Whenever I was working out and got tired and figured I ought to stop, I'd close my eyes and see that list in the locker room without my name on it... that usually got me going again."**
>
> **-Michael Jordan**

7

How Purpose Influences Your Way of Thinking

There are several differences between a person driven by purpose and a person who is yet to find purpose. The most significant among these differences is the direction. A person with purpose, unlike a person without a purpose, has a direction, and this profoundly influences how they approach everything. The way they think and act, are hugely influenced by their purpose.

A simple example is a person who has found purpose in the medical field. This person, because of their purpose, feels obligated to take certain actions that will help fulfill their purpose. They feel a strong need to spend hours reading and preparing for exams in the medical field. These actions are a result of the thought that failure is not an option.

This separates them from a person without purpose and only goes into the medical field for the sake of it. Such a person is not very motivated to take actions that will ensure success because there is no purpose driving them.

Having a strong purpose also makes you more aware of the need to assess the consequences of your actions before doing them. Every action you take could affect your goals negatively or positively.

When you are driven by your purpose, you become more cautious not to do things without thinking deeply about them, and consequently you feel in your mind you are choosing to live a safer life because of the clarity that your purpose has given to you.

Your purpose gives you a clear mind to weigh your available options and choose what you believe to be the best option after critical evaluation.

Let us look at Marie's story, how she found purpose, and what options she considered before her purpose

8

The Story Continues

Marie's first day at Harvard University went better than she expected. Almost everybody she met wanted to speak with the girl on crutches. She could not even count the number of people she had shaken hands with and the number of students who had hugged her, maybe a bit too cordially, that day.

Even a new dear friend Saki from Christian fellowship (a church she started attending after her mother's death), who was helping her with her bags, could not resist making sly comments and funny faces every time a random guy felt the need to say hi to her. She even encountered a random lady who gave her a very unexpected warm embrace after a short conversation. She knew she could not have asked for a better first day in college.

After Saki bid Marie goodbye and Marie was done getting to know her new roommate (an Asian-American who also looked like she was in her early 20s too), she began to drift away in her thoughts. She reflected on the events that had taken place over the past few days and how things had played out in her preparation to resume.

She had contemplated committing suicide several times in the past years, but the urge to end it all seemed to increase in the past month. She had also considered inflicting harm on her father or even killing him when next she saw him.

One morning, she sat up in bed wondering where it had all gone wrong for her family and what preventive measures could have been taken by her parents in order to avoid reality as terrible as this.

Her mother had gotten pregnant while she was in high school at the age of 16, and her father, a high school dropout who was pursuing a career in music had borrowed money from the wrong group of guys promising to repay when he, in his words, becomes "**a mainstream artist**". He never could repay it.

Marie was borne by a woman who was quickly and irredeemably becoming addicted to all sorts of hard drugs that one could lay their hands on. She was born to a man notorious for his illegal activities. You name a petty crime; her father had committed it at some point.

Now, she was also at a point in her life when she had to decide on what she wanted to do with her life. But what were her options? Seeing how her mother lived and died, she knew that taking or selling drugs was not what she wanted for herself. Her father's life was also a lesson to her, not to take certain risks, especially ones you may never recover from.

She knew she did not want her own kids to hate her and would never forgive herself if she became a junkie!

After a long period of brainstorming and reflection, Marie realized that her environment was a huge contributor to the reality she was born into and had negatively influenced the young people that grew up in it.

Although, she obviously noticed that people who attended the fellowship in the neighborhood tended to live better lives and seemed to have a better grasp of what was ideal for themselves. When she met Saki, Marie was fascinated by the big dreams she had and wondered what made an Asian-American like her have such confidence in herself.

Saki had told her about a spoken word poem she heard about how your reality can only be shaped by how you limit your thinking. That was the day Marie made the biggest gains in shaking off the suicidal thoughts that had dogged her for so long. She made up her mind not to let her current reality prevent her from seeing the options she had to choose from.

Marie decided that her purpose in life would be to help unfortunate children who grew up in her neighborhood and similar neighborhoods like her own, to get the possibility to choose and make choices while having the opportunity not to end up like most of their elder folks from the community who in her eyes were now giving people of her color a bad name.

Marie made up her mind that to achieve this purpose, she would have to live a life of discipline and focus. She decided that she was going to get her degree, stay away from people whose goals were not in line with her purpose, and most importantly, she told herself that she would refuse to allow the color of her skin or her disability to hinder her from achieving her purpose.

From Marie's story, we see a lady who found her purpose in the reality she was born into and despite the numerous challenges she faced such as losing one of her own legs at an early age, having financial problems and eating from hand to mouth, losing a mother and so on.

She was able to find purpose in a dream to help people who were born into families like hers, and environments that had negative impacts on innocent children like her own, to take control of their fates and create a reality that they wanted for themselves.

However, finding her purpose was not all that she did. She also knew that she had to weigh the options that were available to her in order to achieve her purpose. She compared the life she wanted for herself to the one her parents had and knew that to fulfill her purpose she would have to consider options that were very much different from the steps that her parents took.

After weighing her options, she picked what she believed to be her best option and went on to set steppingstones for herself as regards discipline, focus, what to do and what not to do with herself. These decisions she made are as a result of what, in this book, we could refer to as the art of optional thinking

9

Fear

"Do not be afraid; our fate cannot be taken from us; it is a gift."

-Dante Alighieri

Before heading out to the next chapter, let's talk about fear. The above words by Dante are the words you might want to consider reciting to yourself while you're experiencing fear and deciding what you want for yourself in the near or distant future.

That is, every time fear seems to be holding you back from finding your path or choosing your endgame, you should remember Dante's words. It is not unnatural to feel a bit of fear when dealing with the unknown.

Everyone gets scared occasionally, and it is nothing to be ashamed of because it is part of what makes us a human being. However, it is the constant reminder that you are not comfortable living in your current reality, that should push you to refuse that reality and decide for yourself the new reality you really want.

Several men in the past have confessed to being repeatedly scared in their lives. However, the many who were able to overcome their fears all tend to agree that overtime, they realized that if they submit to their fears, then they will be stuck in the present and unable to move and find a purpose for their lives.

A good example of a man who refused to let fear get a hold of him is the popular soccer player, Cristiano Ronaldo. In an interview about one of the most acrobatic goals he ever scored, he was asked whether he was scared he would miss.

He responded that he was scared, he knew he could have missed, he knew he could have landed badly and sustained an injury, and he also knew there was a possibility he could have scored. He said, although he was scared, he also knew that nothing comes without risk.

The worst decisions in life we make are always the ones we make out of fear

- **Sherilyn Kenyon**

In another interview, he recounted that he had tried a similarly acrobatic move to score a goal while representing his national team in a soccer match. According to him, the ball only hit the bar, then the goal line and was not given as a goal. This experience of failing at a similar moment must have contributed to the fear he felt this time around.

However, Cristiano Ronaldo, who is known for his insatiable desire to keep winning, knew he had to take calculated risks such as that one at various points in his life if his purpose of becoming one of the greatest soccer players ever in the history of the sport is to be achieved.

Cristiano is not alone in this, it is the same for everyone, including you. Everyone should have a purpose that drives them towards excellence and never let uncertainties distract them from their purpose.

You could choose to let the maybes and the unknowns scare you or you could decide to envision a new reality for yourself and work hard towards achieving that purpose.

Many people have been in Cristiano's shoes, some missed, some got injured, some did not even try to hit the ball at all, and others just took the shot. Which of these people will you be? Fear is normal, but never let fear stop you from making that decision towards your purpose

III
Choices

"Your beliefs affect your choices. Your choices shape your actions. Your actions determine your results. The future you create depends upon the choices you make and the actions you take today"

-Roy T. Bennett

Choices are a crucial part of our lives. Everyone has choices they need to make at various points of their lives, but what are the reasons for these choices? Why do we make these choices? Knowing why we make these choices will play a significant role in helping us make the best ones.

Some people make certain choices because of the environment they come from, the kind of education they got, the kind of family they grew up in, or even because of the kinds of friends they kept.

All our choices are always consciously or subconsciously influenced by something: a belief, a bad habit, addiction, knowledge, misinformation, and so on. Roy T. Bennett's words about choices really summed it all up.

"You are not the victim of the world, but rather the master of your own destiny. It is your choices and decisions that determine your destiny."

-Roy T. Bennett

It is common knowledge that the choices we made in our past, played a huge role in making us who we are today, and the choices we make today, could possibly make us who we become tomorrow.

However, having the ability to make choices, implies that we have the option to choose what we think is best at the time of making those choices. Having this ability to choose is what makes optional thinking possible.

Most would agree that they believe they will eventually have to make a choice at some point in time in your life. This means that they also believe that they have more than one option at a time, and for them to even consider these options to choose from, it would have to imply that these options are possibilities, and if it is possible, it indeed exists.

For instance, if you had a goal of leaving the country, your options on how to travel would have to be the ones that not only exist but are also an available possibility to you. At the end of the day, you must decide whether to travel by land, by air or by sea.

As a person, you get a sense that your reality is what you have experienced and seen until now. That it is what got you to what - is your current reality. More importantly, it got you to your present time in your life which is now, is only just your starting point.

Your purpose on the other hand is where you want to be, or better put, it is your destination. Or, as we will call it several times in this book; your endgame. To get to your endgame, you must make informed choices that lean towards your purpose. In other words, you must make decisions that will help materialize your purpose.

For instance, your purpose may be that you want to graduate from high school. The next step would be to make choices that lean towards that. You have several options available to you such as paying tuition, studying hard, partying, attending classes and so on. Considering what your options are carefully before making your choice is a major aspect of the optional thinking method.

The greatest question ever asked that relates to the choice in my opinion is a question that was asked by Shakespeare in his play *Hamlet*. "**To be, or not to be**". Through that expression, Shakespeare considers the options before him, which one could more than assume was suicide or staying alive, and with these options comes a need to make a choice.

Throughout your life, there will always be a time to make a choice, and those choices can play a crucial role in determining what the outcome of your life will be. It is necessary to admit that no one knows what is right or wrong until the outcome, but it is also necessary to know that if your choice is not to act at all, you are still making a choice which will lead to an outcome as well.

Going by these crucial parts of optional thinking, if choices influence your future reality, then you need to start making them now, in the present. That is, if you intend to move on from your past reality and start choosing the options available to you towards your endgame.

The probability of an outcome being the way you intended it to be when you carefully considered the possibilities seems more likely when they are led by your purpose. You may choose to read for a test or not and still pass the test. But you are more likely to pass if you read it. No one ever knows what the future is; however, it is advisable to make our choices based on what is most probable to lead you to the outcome that you want. By doing this, you become confident and have a stronger assurance thing will turn out the way you want them to. Knowing you took the major steps necessary to achieving that outcome you are looking for when making choices that will lead to your purpose.

By making choices based on how much it leans towards your purpose, it removes fear and doubts from your mind.

Choices are like an in-between map of where you are starting from and where you are heading to. It is also the fuel that helps you go on even when you feel too tired to keep going. It is easier to keep going when you know where you are going and how to get there.

With a purpose in mind, you know that the next choices you make must bring you closer to the set purpose. When you feel that the choice you are about to make is the right one for you, it spurs you to keep going and gives you the feeling that you are more in control of your life.

There is a saying that God gave us two wonderful gifts: *the ability of choice and the ability to reason.* Everybody gets a sense of control and feels free to live their life when they are making choices for themselves based on their own ability to think. That is why optional thinking could be considered a good approach to achieving your purpose because although you have no control over the unknown, which is the future, optional thinking will help you prepare and move from your reality towards your purpose.

Therefore, in this book, we identify reality as past, purpose as future, and choice as present. We use choice as a vehicle that takes us from reality to our purpose or, from our past to our future.

In life, so many circumstances come and then you realize that there are certain things in your life that are not under your control, such as what family you are born into, being involved in a car crash, being in a building when a fire starts or a global virus outbreak. But the one thing you can control is how you choose, and what you choose to do or not to do when adversity comes. And adversity does come, in one shape or another, into every life.

What you need to do is not complain and wallow in self-pity. When things go wrong, or bad things happen, or circumstances are less than ideal, you need to concentrate. Control what you can, in order to move from where you are to where you want to be in the near or distant future.

It is not uncommon for people to ask you to "**find your why**." Once you find your why you can start choosing to get to your why, that is, when you find your purpose then you can start choosing to get to your purpose. Remember, you cannot choose anything if it is not an available option. Therefore, optional thinking becomes possible when you bring your options to your table, that is, when you make things that are possible, available or existent for you to choose.

When you make your options available, then they become possible, and then you can take full advantage of those present possibilities and choose the options that lean towards your purpose. When you are true to yourself and your expectations are in line with your intentions when making a choice, it gives you the confidence to face what is on the other side of any wall.

It helps you look forward to moving on. The great thing about this approach is that whatever the outcome, it gives a sense that you are more at ease to accept the outcome because you know your choices brought you to where you are now, and you are headed in a direction towards your endgame.

> "Think a hundred times before you take a decision, but once that decision is taken; stand by it as one man"
>
> -Muhammad Ali

Optional thinking makes the process of making a choice a reasonable one and a logical one towards our purpose. The aim is to build up hope and faith in our purpose because when you are too worried about something, it could slow down the decision-making and prevent you from making choices you feel is the best choice at various times.

Even when fear or doubt prevents you from acting, you have still made a choice, which may not be the best option at the time. However, when you are confident in your purpose and begin applying the approach of optional thinking, you could decide not to act, and it would be because you believed that was the most logical or the best option to go with at the time.

In the first chapter, we talked about the analogy of skinning a cat, and the same applies here.

There are always different choices, you just must become aware of your choices and make them an option available for yourself so they can turn into a great possibility towards your endgame. When an opportunity comes knocking, we must choose to be positioned to notice it and choose to open the door. Choices give you a sense of accountability, for example, you could decide that you want to lose weight. Now the process of losing that weight begins and unless you have a medical condition that affects your weight, the choices you make from there on will determine how much weight you really lose. It is well documented that in most cases, weight is tied to your diet and lifestyle. These are things you can control.

In order to achieve this weight loss purpose, you could make choices such as watching what you eat, learning new ways to lose weight, and then acting on what you learned. In optional thinking, you must weigh all your available options to know exactly which ones are advantageous to your purpose and which ones are not.

When you have finally defined your purpose, the steppingstones it takes becomes motivated by your purpose. Choices such as working out, reading books, eating certain kinds of foods that contribute to your weight loss, visiting gyms, eating out less or just preparing your very own wholesome meals - all these things are basically done in order to get to the endgame. The point here is that our choices are like a roadmap, and they guide us to our endgame.

10

Choice and Purpose

"Destiny is not fate, it's navigation"

-Richie Norton

Earlier on, we described the choice as a vehicle that takes us from where we are now to where we want to be. We also referred to the choice as the roadmap that leads us to our endgame. These metaphors are used to describe the relationship between choice and purpose are simply a way of conveying the message that our choices are what determine whether our purpose in life is fulfilled.

The importance of the relationship between choices and purpose cannot be overemphasized in this book, as it is practically the part of optional thinking that propels you to want to keep moving forward.

On the journey to fulfilling purpose, there are always steppingstones that we will encounter and accomplish along the way, these steppingstones are carefully set up by you to lead you to the destination. This is where choices come to play.

Your purpose is like your very own journey and therefore requires you to make decisions for yourself to choose how you want to accomplish that journey and what approach you want to take to get to your endgame. Optional thinking offers you the approach of considering your options carefully and choosing what you feel is the best options available that lean towards your purpose. These choices you make are the steppingstones that lift you towards achieving your purpose.

In other words, the more you make choices, which would be the best available option at each point, the closer you get to your endgame.

Choices are like the stairs that lead you up to the next floor, and for you to get to that floor, you need to take it one step at a time until you get to your destination. The analogy of the staircase may sound quite simple, but you only need to apply it to your journey. Let us apply it to the story of Mr. Tom who was in an accident that affected his back and consequently affected his ability to walk or even sit up.

This is Mr. Tom's present reality, but the doctor keeps reminding him that he has seen patients go through similar ordeals and still regain their ability to walk.

However, none of these patients achieved this without working towards it. Mr. Tom has been presented with a future reality by the doctor, but it is up to him to make those choices that will help him achieve that endgame of being able to walk again.

Like in the case of the staircase, Mr. Tom must climb each stair individually making the decision not to stop after the first or second or third step, but to keep going until he gets to the top floor which is his endgame. However, he must make the choice to start the journey first before accomplishing the smaller steppingstones that will surely lift him towards accomplishing the larger purpose of being able to walk again.

Once he makes the first choice to start then it could become relatively easier to go through the process knowing that this could be a way, he will get the possibility of not only to sit up but walking again.

11

Reasoning

"Who cares about the crowded, broad road? I'll walk the single plank bridge into the night"

-Mo Dao Zu Shi

As stated at the beginning of this chapter, the process of optional thinking requires you to make decisions based on reason. There are always several options available to a person who has a purpose, however, the right mindset to approach this would be to carefully examine the options and choose the one that leans towards your endgame.

This pattern of reasoning is what allows optional thinking to be a productive approach. Your choices should not be motivated by what most people tend to do when they find themselves in a similar position or what is popular among your peers and others.

It should be motivated by your very own purpose. You should always try to keep in mind that everyone has their very own agenda for their life and therefore, other people's roadmap that works for them will not always work for you and vice versa. No matter how similar your purpose may be.

An example of someone having this sort of reasoning is four-time NBA champion LeBron James. When making decisions, there were probably a lot of different reasons that one could possibly assume he considered before making his choice to take his talents to south beach; his family and how it helps contribute to his success as a basketball player. Let's assume these were some of the key factors that made LeBron's move away from the Cleveland Cavaliers to join the Miami Heat.

We know for sure that one reason he made the decision was his confidence in his abilities. His exact words were

"When you feel like you are really good at your craft, I think it's always great to be around other great minds and that's why I have left".

He went on to say in another interview that his ultimate reason for any decision he makes is to keep winning and to stay happy.

At the time, there were a lot of negative reactions to Lebron James leaving the Cavaliers, but he made his decision and was able to win two NBA Championships with the Miami Heat in 2012 and 2013. Furthermore, he made another decision and reasoning to return to the Cleveland Cavaliers, ultimately capturing an NBA championship with the Cleveland Cavaliers in 2016.

This success after leaving his old team is proof that he was sure of the choice he was making at the time and proof that when you are sure an option is the best one to achieve your purpose, then you should take that option irrespective of what people think or say because at the end of the day it is your life to live.

12
How to Make Choices

There are a lot of things to do before making a choice, and here are a few useful tips:

1. BE AWARE OF YOUR OPTIONS

"The world is not a problem; the problem is your unawareness."

- Bhagwan Shree Rajneesh

In the process of making your choices, you need to always remind yourself that there are several options available to you.

This awareness of your many options is what allows you to be more informed before making a choice, it also enables you to choose from all your available options, the one that you believe to be the best choice at every decision-making point in your life. Lack of awareness is one of many reasons why people tend to make choices ending in what one would consider a negative outcome.

Recently, schools have begun to organize seminars for all their students, incoming and outgoing. Many students come into school not knowing the numerous options that are available to them and therefore only make a choice based on the limited knowledge that they have.

Some decide to major in the arts because their parents also were in the arts back in their school days when clearly, they are not suited for the arts. This decision is a myopic one. It is important that a person is aware of the range of opportunities they have. This awareness brings with it the comfort of being able to choose properly what leans best towards your purpose.

2. KNOW YOUR STRENGTHS

"The awareness of our own strength makes us modest"

-Paul Cezanne

In every sporting competition, every coach has the desire to win every game. However, the method one coach uses differs from the next coach. This is because the coach knows the strengths of his team and makes his decisions that are in line with his teams' strengths.

Also, a coach knows the weaknesses of his team and tries to avoid methods that reveal his team's weaknesses. In some cases, the coach goes through the process of eradicating the weaknesses of the team if possible. This is the case for everyone who has a purpose and hopes to achieve them.

Like these coaches, you must know your weaknesses and try to avoid making choices that reveal them. Likewise, it is important that you know your strengths and choose from your available options, the one that compliments your strengths that leads toward your endgame.

3. KNOW YOUR PURPOSE

This is arguably the most important factor to consider when making a choice. Your purpose is the endgame and should therefore determine the kind of choices you should make. If your purpose is to be a football player, then your choice of food, lifestyle, and even the kind of relationships you keep must lean towards your purpose.

There are always several options that are available to you at every point in your life; however, you must only make choices that will make your purpose become a reality. In the previous chapter, we explored how having a purpose makes all your choices calculated.

When you have a steppingstone or when you have an endgame to achieve, you become more careful about the kind of choices you make and consequently you try to choose only the best choices you feel are for you after critically weighing the options that are available. In a discussion between a soccer player and a reporter, he was asked why he did not get angry or retaliate at a player who seemed to have kicked him while the game was in play.

His response was simple. The team had a goal to win a trophy that year and knowing how important he was to the team in achieving that goal, he had made the choice not to allow anyone to get him ejected from the game. His purpose was the reason for the choices he made.

4. BE WILLING TO ACCEPT CHANGE

You will find that it is necessary to let things go; simply for the reason that they are heavy"

-C. JoyBell C.

Just as we mentioned earlier, there are times when a coach may see the need to make corrections that will help solve some weaknesses in his team. The coach may see these corrections as the only way to build a team that will become unbeatable in the future. This can only be applied to our process of making choices if we are willing to undergo some serious changes.

Denzel Washington played a character named Robert Mccall in a movie titled *The Equalizer*. In the movie, a colleague of Roberts had a dream of working as security personnel at a factory where they both worked. There was however a slight problem, this colleague weighed too much and could not meet the requirements for the position.

During the movie, Robert helped his colleague to realize that he had many options, he could quit, he could keep hoping, or he could put in calculated efforts into trying to lose weight. These efforts would include a change in diet, undergoing rigorous workout sessions and most importantly, discipline.

This colleague accepted the need to undergo a change and after choosing to do what was necessary, he lost enough weight and passed the test to become security personnel at the factory.

The journey towards achieving your purpose would require making some choices that will require you to endure some changes in your body, your lifestyle, the kinds of things you do in your spare time, the kind of friends you hang out with, and even the number of hours you get at night to sleep. However, these changes are chosen to fulfill your purpose.

13
The Story Pursues

After many weeks of preparing, the next day was Marie's final exams and she had never been this enthusiastic about anything in her entire life. She was so confident about how the exam would go that she could barely wait to get into the exam hall and put in her best.

She had discovered her purpose some years back and had ensured that every choice she made from that day would bring her closer to her purpose of becoming a helper for kids who had rough starts to life like her.

That night while lying on her bed, reflecting on the choices she had to make over the past 4 years, she could only smile at how easy they now seem to have been. For any other kid, it would have been too difficult to take the steps she took or to find the courage to keep moving, but looking back, it all now seemed surprisingly easy for her.

Although from time to time she had a worry or two; she did not let them blind her from seeing the bigger picture; She knew what the endgame was and knew all she had to do was choose the available options about which she was feeling greatly confident in and that leaned towards her endgame.

Today she was top of her class and had just been informed by the head of her department that companies were already lining up to pay for her services. The choices she made were already being rewarded.

When many of her colleagues dropped out of college for several of their own reasons, she chose not to, because her purpose would be endangered by that single action alone. Though the thought of dropping out came once after several waves of racially motivated abuse that she had to face, she had to realize for herself that dropping out would not be a reasonable steppingstone option that would lead her closer to her endgame and would only make these sometimes-anonymous attackers the winner in her story.

When people tried to convince her to slow down on her reading to make room for parties, vacations, going to the movies and so on, she was resilient. She knew those were some of the available options for her, but she also knew they did not lean towards her endgame at this point in her life.

Overtime, she had to cut ties with so many friends because of the massive differences between their endgame and how they chose to go about it. On one occasion, Sophia, her roommate accused her of being proud and judgmental of people who just wanted to have fun and not just work all the time like her.

On several occasions, Marie had refused to go out to late-night parties with Sophia and this had led Sophia into making these wrong assumptions about Marie. Marie was so upset when she heard this and could not resist getting into a heated argument with her roommate that day.

Marie had to make it clear that she has never condemned anyone's approach to anything, and that she only chose the approach she has chosen because she believed it was the best option available to her if she were to achieve her own purpose. Her purpose was personal to her and refused to let anyone dictate how she chose to move towards it and she in turn would not force her choices on others, just give her truth, her reality, why she chooses her path and how it works for her.

If there was anything she had learned from the life of her parents, it was that the choices you made in your past could determine your present, and the choices you make today, could determine what your future reality will be. This was why she knew that she had to be careful while weighing her options and be more rational while making her choices.

For her, trying to please her friends by making the decisions that was not in line with her endgame was not the rational thing to do and she chose never to do that.

People always accused her of being over-confident and never showing the normal fear that every student would show before exams, during the exams and even when the results are about to be released.

She wished she could help them understand that this confidence was not baseless. It was only normal that a person who has only made decisions that lean towards her purpose fill with the confidence and belief she is going to pass going into her final exams.

Especially when the odds are in favor of her because of the choices she has made in the past to study and utterly understand what the exams could be all about for herself. She had never seen the questions before and had never written at this level of exams before, but she had ensured that she did everything she believed she needed to do to not just pass but pass with a high score.

While her friends slept, partied, played, and did the normal things that students would do during their leisure times, she read at the school library and attended tutorials for whatever courses she was having a hard time with. She had weighed her available options that year and chose the option of reading every book on the syllabus from cover to cover. This was the reason for her confidence.

She, like all students, had worries at first. She had never picked an option as tough as this. She had limited time and a lot of books to read, and this made her a bit worried that she may not be able to fulfill this steppingstone she had set for herself. She had always had this problem as a kid. Worrying was one of the few things she always struggled with, to overcome and although it reduced over the years, it was back again in her final year.

However, with focus and trust in her ability, she chose to stick to her plan. She knew that if she chooses not to attend some of the little things going on around the school like social outings and other non-academic-related activities, she will have the available time to be able to achieve her goal of studying every book on the syllabus for the final year exams, and she did.

Marie knew where she was heading and was not going to let the worries or fears of just one exam hold her back from achieving her endgame to pass. Journalism was just one of the steppingstones she needed to achieve her purpose and she knew she still had a long way to go after the final exams. She had made many choices, and still had many more to make.

14
Worries

"In any moment of decision, the best thing you can do is the right thing. The worst thing you can do is nothing."

-Theodore Roosevelt

Most people tend to get worried whenever they are about to make a choice. Most of the time when people must make some type of choice they tend to hesitate, and it is because they are worried. This worrying is usually a result of their fear of whether the choice they are about to make is the right one or the wrong one.

Another common reason for worrying is that people are always bothered about whether they are good enough to take the action they are about to take.

But you should realize that the best way to overcome worry, is to remind yourself that if you are too worried to act, by not acting, you have already made a choice. That choice is the decision not to act. When a person is being fueled by a purpose, you should be able to overcome any kind of worry. Try applying the reasoning method of optional thinking that was recommended to you in the previous section.

When you are careful with the decisions you make and only make choices based on how well they lean towards your endgame, your worries reduce. This is because you are aware that your choices are not misguided and more importantly, that your choices are motivated by a purpose that you want to achieve.

Joseph Cossman once said,

"If you want to test your memory, try to recall what you were worrying about one year ago today."

This quote by Joseph is one way of saying that worrying does not actually solve anything and neither does it change anything. All you can really do at that point in your life is make the choice and cross each bridge one at a time when you get to them.

Some time ago, out of curiosity, a boy once asked his father what the future held for him. The father asked his son not to be worried about what the future had in store for him. Father gave the son advice that stuck with him till he became a man.

"Son, do not worry for tomorrow, rather prepare yourself for the tomorrow that you want".

He understood that his father was telling him that worrying for tomorrow is not helpful, but that working hard to make tomorrow a good one is what matters.

As you will discover from the story of Marie later, she has the problem of worrying about the factors surrounding her choice. However, she was able to summon courage from within and from the realization that her choice to act becomes way better than not acting at all.

This is a mentality that you should have if you want to overcome any kind of worry that may arise at any point of decision-making in the journey to your endgame.

IV
Optional Thinking

"When your intentions are in line with your expectations, you are being true to yourself"

-Donell Edmond

In the first chapter of this book, we talked about reality as a thing of the past. We talked about the need to understand who you are, what you have been through, the effects that your experiences have on your current reality, what your strengths and limitations are, accepting this reality, and finally getting to a point where you decide that moving forward and never going back to that same reality is the best option for you.

There is a statement that I usually say that I believe compliments the idea that was being conveyed in chapter one.

The stage of accepting your reality and choosing to move on is also the stage where you have to say to yourself, **"when I do this, I expect certain results."** This means that it is the stage you get to, where you decide to take actions that will help you move on from your past reality. What makes you choose to accept your reality and move on to a true one, is your readiness to act on that choice. This is the foundation for optional thinking.

> **"You can't lay hold of what you want in life while still holding onto the thing you had…"**
>
> -Donell Edmond

We also talked about doubts and how these doubts come from the knowledge of our limitations. Like in the case of Marie, who had doubts about how to move on and whether she was good enough for the university.

She had these doubts because of her disability and the color of her skin. We went on to explain that to move on, you need to minimize these doubts, while beginning to maximize your belief in yourself and in the possibility of a better future. Moving on can truly be possible if you get to a point where your belief in yourself and self-confidence outweighs your doubts and fears.

> **"Get to a point where you don't want to go back so you can move forward."**
>
> -Donell Edmond

When you believe in yourself, it allows you to accept your reality, believing that your reality is the way it is for a reason. It helps you get to the point where you can gather enough strength to take that first step, which is moving on, never looking back, and staying true to your intentions. Doubts bring excuses, but confidence helps you look past these excuses.

"Life is too short. Most people would say this statement is true. But I would rather see it as false. Life is all about living, and living is the longest thing that a person will do in their lifetime. So why not just live your life"

-Donell Edmond

In the second chapter, we discussed the purpose. After making the final choice to move forward from your past reality, we discussed the purpose of why having a destination in mind is important to moving on to your new reality. When you decide to move forward, you need to ask yourself where exactly you are moving to. You need to know where you are headed and, more particularly, why you are heading in that direction.

This is where purpose comes into play. The purpose is your reason for being, your reason for living, your reason for moving forward, your reason for trying to be a better person. Your purpose is the reason you are ready to go into the unknown. We also mentioned the fear of the unknown.

When a person decides to move on and discovers their purpose, there is also the fear that things may not go as planned. This fear makes a person want to protect themselves from a negative outcome. However, there is a disadvantage that also comes with this fear, and that is the fact that it prevents you from moving forward.

There is no way a person can move forward into the possibility of a better reality if they are built up with fear of the unknown. But there is a strong possibility to overcome this fear when you keep your focus on your purpose. Your purpose gives you a mental map and with this mental map, you now have that sense of direction and more importantly, you now begin the journey of discovering how to get there.

You will find that knowing where you are going, helps to give you the confidence to keep moving forward. When your confidence begins to grow and maximize inside you by knowing where you are going and knowing you have the means to get there, it also helps to minimize your fear.

Even when you take the wrong turn, or you find yourself in a situation where you do not want to be, you still will not be afraid because you know your endgame, and you only need to do the things that will take you there. The fact that there is an endgame is what helps you face the unknown with confidence. This is what we identify as hope.

Hope is the cornerstone and the core of optional thinking. We want to move forward. We want to get to our endgame. The whole reason for discussing our current state of being, that is our reality, and talking about purpose is because we want to create a huge consciousness in our minds that brings hope of a better reality. That is, a consciousness of moving forward through optional thinking.

Irrespective of any outcome at different stages of our journey to our purpose, there needs to be a consciousness of moving on and not giving up. This consciousness is born of the hope that shows us there is a possibility of a better reality waiting around the corner for us.

"The choices we made yesterday made us who we are today. Figure out who you want to be tomorrow, so you can make choices today and be that person tomorrow"

-Donell Edmond

To get to our purpose, which is the endgame, we must make some choices, and this was discussed in the third chapter. It is like the case of a person who is trying to get somewhere. You have a destination already, but to get to that destination, you must make choices on what routes to take, what to take with you, your means of getting there, do you want to go alone, and so on.

All these are choices that one needs to make in order to get to the desired location. We also talked about worrying in the third chapter. We observed that one common thing that comes up when people are about to make choices, is that they begin to worry.

They worry about whether their choice is the right one; they worry about whether they are good enough to go to the next level of their journey. We went on to explain that there is always hope if we keep making those choices, whereas, worrying too much about something that has not happened yet or trying to be right about the possibilities we are faced with can significantly reduce your chances of moving forward.

Even if you make the wrong choice, you are still enthusiastic to keep moving and try again because of your faith and the hope with belief that there is a better reality for yourself, and this is truly a possibility as long as you are alive.

"What's the difference between a fool and a wise man? Outcome"

-Donell Edmond

You know what your reality is, you have identified what your purpose is, and now you are at the point where you need to make choices to move closer to that purpose. The point here is not that making the best choice guarantees the results and outcomes you want. Of course not; no one knows the future. Things go wrong. We live in a world of social and political problems that affect our lives, and over which we have little control. The point is that we stand a much better chance of ending up where we want to be if we make choices that align with our purpose, and if we move forward with faith towards that end.

Optional thinking, when broken down into simple pieces, ultimately embodies an idea that you need to make choices. In optional thinking, you are brought to the consciousness that there are always several options that are available to you and all you need to do is to decide which option to choose, with your mindset on the fact that you want to move forward.

> **"Knowing your reality can help you identify your purpose. Making choices towards your purpose can help make it your new reality"**
>
> -Donell Edmond

Always remind yourself that there are a range of options open to you. Where the options appear limited, step back and look again. Sometimes we are too near to the problems and from that vantage point, can't really see options. Sometimes the options aren't there yet, but we can take steps to create them. You owe it to yourself to take advantage of the best option that takes you towards your endgame. This is your responsibility and no one else's.

Optional thinking gives you a mind-set that if your purpose is possible then in order to obtain it you should try to put yourself in a place where if these possibilities come knocking at the door, you are in the position to open it. Optional thinking teaches you to learn to never leave things that have to do with your very own purpose to chance. You should work towards choosing those options that draw you closer to what you have set out to achieve.

> "You don't have to waste time getting ready when the time comes if you were ready before. Position yourself so when opportunities knock you can open the door."
>
> -Donell Edmond

To achieve your own personal endgame, we must work towards getting the existing information that we need for the steppingstones towards our endgame. This information could be in books, in people's experiences, in schools, through word of mouth, and so on.

Through this method of reasoning, we can go on to filter the information we have consumed and choose that which we think is the best option. I always say that God's greatest gift to man is our ability to choose and the ability to reason.

In other words, God has empowered us with not only the ability to think, but also with several options that can be made available to us through the choices that we make.

As a 38-year-old, I always try to use my reality as an example when explaining optional thinking to people. There is always the choice on whether to live or to die and if your choice is to live, then comes the big question which I love to ask people, **"Why not live your best life?"**

Know why you want to live and go on seeking all the possibilities life has to offer and try making choices that will help you get to your endgame by achieving your reason **"Why!"** Optional thinking is an approach that has worked for me in my life and that is why I have chosen to share it with the world.

I have met with a lot of people in my lifetime, discussed several topics and debatable issues with them, such as how do they identify purpose, their understanding of reality, and several choices they made in their life that resulted in outcomes that were positive and negative. I have even had online conversations, asking people for help to obtain information that pertained to certain areas of life. All this was to help me achieve my purpose of writing this book with real-life proof that it works. In simple words, it was my choices that brought me to this point of achieving my endgame.

I knew my endgame, and after considering the options that were readily available to me, I made choices that gradually brought me closer to my endgame.

This book is my endgame, and I authored it because I want it to become my new reality. At some point, I was worried that no one would like it, also the fear that I may never complete this book.

But then I chose to apply optional thinking to this project process and chose to believe in the possibility of a positive reality for myself as an author of a book, which in this case, is a completed project that gives people what I believe to be a practical, common sense formula to help them live their best life, and to do so despite past trauma or oppressive circumstances. I mean for it to be a book to help people build belief, keep faith and remain hopeful.

I am not asserting that what I am presenting to you is the solution to every problem. But I sincerely believe that optional thinking is a very handy tool that can help anyone solve the core problems of their lives. I am trying to put the mindset of optional thinking into words, so it can be an option for you that you will hopefully end up applying to your own reality as you see fit.

As a child, when I was growing up, there was a saying that my pastor always used to close out the church service that stuck with me always.

"If every soul helps save one soul, then every soul can be saved"

-Reverend David Watts

From this statement, I was able to get a personal understanding by writing this book and helping people achieve personal growth and trying to obtain the possibility of a better version of themselves. I have been able to share with people an important knowledge that has brought me to a place which I have identified as a piece of happiness. By sharing this happiness with people, it is a strong possibility this book can bring a sense of happiness to someone who reads and applies it to their way of life.

After reading this book, if you too experience this "**Happiness**", then you could share it with someone else as well. With this, we can spread happiness to everyone in the world by helping them find the hope that can possibly create a positive reality, future, and present. As we can see now, with hope comes happiness.

15

The Optional Thinking Mindset: Hope, Belief and Faith

We have discussed the importance of reality, purpose, and choice in the previous concept of Optional Thinking. But it is necessary to reiterate that the right mindset that a person needs when using optional thinking is that of belief, hope and faith.

Faith here does not necessarily have to be from a religious perspective. As a person who has an endgame in mind, it is necessary that you always hope for the best results. This is not to say that all your choices will be the right ones or that things will always go as planned, but with hope, you know that even when things go wrong, your endgame is still a possibility, and you still have options from which to choose that will help make that endgame a reality.

Belief and faith go hand in hand. Over the years, many studies have proven that one of the key things that keep people going in their journey towards success is their strong belief in something.

For many, it is their unflinching belief in themselves, for some, it is their belief in a mantra or a philosophy, for some it is their belief in the training or education they have received, and for some, it is their belief in a supernatural being.

Talking about belief in one's training or education reminds me of an NBA player who is known for his passion and work ethic, Jamal Murray. Trained by his father in the cold city of Kitchener, Ohio Canada, under the ideals of Bruce Lee, Jamal Murray developed a mentality that his training which has been compared to Navy Seal training was to prepare him to dominate the NBA.

This belief in his training is the reason he is always so confident about every shot he takes and every move he makes in his NBA career. This belief has helped him become a fast-rising star in the NBA and he is gradually getting closer to achieving his endgame of leaving his name on the historical records of the NBA.

Having true faith in God is another foundation that helps believers make good choices when trying to live in the eye of God and live a righteous and fulfilled life. Denzel Washington, a great American actor, director, and producer told a story about his experience in 1975.

He had just graduated from college with a 1.7 GPA and was sitting in his mother's beauty parlor when he looked in the mirror and saw a woman behind him under the drier. She told him that she had a prophecy for him and that she saw him traveling around the world and speaking to millions of people.

According to Denzel, what she told him that day made him confident to pursue a bigger future for himself. His faith had made him believe in a better reality for himself, and today he has achieved that endgame of becoming a successful man in a lot of ways.

These three key things are part of a mindset that one should have to be able to apply this optional thinking to their lives. With hope, belief and faith, it becomes much easier to face worries, doubts and fear. By maximizing one set will lead to the minimizing of the other set.

This mind-set of always hoping for the best, believing in oneself, and faith in something bigger than yourself, such as God or philosophy or principle, is the way to walk into the unknown and towards your endgame.

16

The Endgame

I've used this term many times in the course of writing this book and I think it's only appropriate that I explain the allusion. I got the word *endgame* from the Avengers movie about Thanos and what he believed to be his purpose.

Thanos believed that the universe was on the brink of extinction, because of overpopulation. The struggle to control the universe's resources led to war, hunger, diseases and so on. He believed that his purpose was to help save the universe from its undoubtedly imminent doom.

Thanos' approach of wiping out half the universe is undoubtedly extreme, but it was the choice of a person who knew what he had to do to achieve his purpose. He must have considered his options and chosen the one that seemed almost certain to prevent the coming end of the universe. This is what endgame means.

Your endgame is your destination, a purpose that you have chosen and intend to work towards achieving.

17

The Story Resumes

The results were out and she had not only aced all her papers, but she was also graduating as the best student in her faculty. The news had been posted on the university's website and had spread like wildfire.

Everyone knew the black one-legged girl who never left the library, but no one could have imagined that Marie would achieve such a feat. What she did not expect were the numerous calls to congratulate her for her achievement.

Marie had spoken to more people in the past week than she had spoken to throughout her time in the university. If only they knew that this was just the first steppingstone that she had taken towards her endgame. It was worth celebrating, but she refused to let it distract her from the next choice she had to make.

A day before her graduation ceremony, while everyone was super excited for her, all she could think about was the project topic she worked on in her final year in school. She had chosen to do her project in the field of journalism and chose the renowned basketball living legend, Lebron James as her player of focus.

Her topic was *The Psychological Influence Of The Media On The Life Of A Current Basketball Player: A Case Study Of Lebron James*. She had done some research into his entire career and was still in awe about so many things she had learned about his journey so far.

Lebron James undoubtedly made several controversial decisions throughout his career that caused stirs amongst fans and even colleagues in the NBA. However, the fear of what people would think of him if he made those decisions never stopped him from going ahead with his decisions. He knew what his endgame was and made choices that helped him achieve it.

Marie wished she could meet him to ask him how he did it. How did he know which options were the best? Which teams to join? When to leave? All these questions had been bothering her for the past weeks until this night.

Marie finally realized what made it easier for Lebron James to make those choices. The secret was that he knew where he was headed and that when a person knows where they are headed, they always know what the next step should be.

Lebron could never have been certain that he would have a successful career as a Miami Heat, but he was willing to believe in himself and in the possibility of a better reality by moving on from his past reality.

Lying in her bed that night, staring at the dress she had ironed for her graduation ceremony the following day, she could not help but think that she was a lot like Lebron James in some ways. Not as an athlete of course, but she was like him in other ways. A few years before, she was also living a reality that she knew was not the best for her.

Her mother had just died as a result of a self-inflicted overdose, her father was a drunk who had the habit of physically abusing her, and she was disabled. But like the NBA legend, she had chosen to accept that reality and to move on from it.

People had told Lebron James that he was making a mistake by leaving the Cleveland Cavaliers, many of them had their opinions of what he should and should not do, and more particularly there were negative comments directed at him by so many people.

Marie had also gone through something similar. Because of her decision to pay absolute attention towards getting good grades and denying herself the chances to attend the social gatherings, people were always very vocal about what they thought of her and her decisions.

Like Lebron, she had been a true victim of negative comments from colleagues, friends, and even people she did not know, but also like Lebron, she did not let these external factors distract her. She knew what her endgame was and knew that she had to make those choices if she wanted to come closer to fulfilling her purpose.

While everyone was filled with frenzy about the upcoming graduation ceremony and the dinner party that always followed, three words kept running through her mind: *"the next steppingstone"*. All Marie could think of now was what the next steppingstone would be.

With her result, she could get a fully paid scholarship to begin her master's program in any university. There were several companies that were ready to offer her high-paying jobs in the country. She had also been approached by one of her professors who asked her to stay behind to serve as an Assistant Lecturer in the faculty.

So many options to choose from, but she knew she had to make only the choice that leaned more towards her endgame.

She had decided on what her purpose would be. She wanted to help kids who grew up in neighborhoods like the one she grew up in. To get them in a position where there are opportunities for them to live a better life, she wanted to help create more options than were available to them in their present situations. She wanted to help them understand their reality didn't have to remain dim, that there is hope for a better future. She wanted to help them understand that it is possible for them to find their endgame and arrange how to get there. She believed they could start working towards a positive reality if given the opportunity. Like her, they could rise above the misery they had seen around them. She had a purpose of helping black kids like her break the stereotype of being born to be criminals, and this can only be accomplished if she attained a position from which she can reach out to these kids.

She had read about another black legend in her second year in the university, Oprah Winfrey. Oprah had been a victim of sexual abuse from the early ages of 9-13 by her uncle, cousin, and family friend. When she was just 14 years old, she became pregnant due to these abuses, and this led her into a breakdown that made her consider committing suicide.

To make matters worse for her, the child died only 2 weeks after he was born due to being born prematurely. She chose to move on from that reality, and after considering her options, chose to bring herself to a new reality by working hard to get a degree at the Tennessee State University.

She had a big break hosting a morning TV show and her career skyrocketed. Today, with the platform she has, she has helped countless young women overcome abuses and helped fight for justice for them.

Marie knew she had not yet achieved her purpose, but like Oprah Winfrey, she knew she was ready to bring her options into existence and make the choices that will help her get to her endgame.

18

Ways to Build Confidence and Overcome Worries

When it comes to making choices, there are always worries that pop in your head at the beginning of the process or even at the last minute. In this section, we would be looking at tips on how to build our confidence during decision-making as seen in real scenarios of various people.

Here are some tips on confidence from the lives of prominent people such as the former First Lady of the United States, Michelle Obama, Will Smith, and Denzel Washington

1. IDENTIFYING YOUR VOICE

In her memoir *Becoming*, Michelle Obama talked about her struggles with adapting to life as a public figure. One of the things that helped her identify her place and purpose in her position was the ability to find her voice amidst all the noise and speak up for herself. Many people are not confident to make choices by themselves because they do not know that they have a right to have a say in their own lives.

Like Marie in our story, we all must learn to block out the many negative voices that surround us and make choices for ourselves. This is important because we are the only ones who truly know our endgame and what options are best suited for us to achieve that endgame. According to Michelle, learning that your voice is not inferior in any sense helps you feel more visible and confident enough to pursue your dreams.

2. DON'T LET OTHER PEOPLE MAKE YOU CHANGE YOUR OPINION OF YOURSELF

This is particularly important to build your confidence. If you pay too much attention to what people think about you, you may lose sight of your endgame. Like Lebron James, Michelle, and our character, Marie, do not let what other people think of you change your belief in yourself and your ability to achieve the purpose that you have set for yourself.

Michelle Obama spoke about when she made the decision to attend Princeton University.

At this time, she was in her senior year in high school and a college counselor told her that she was not Princeton material and that she was reaching higher than she could attain. Michelle Obama did not let this distract her; she went on to apply to Princeton and got in! Like Will Smith said to his son in the movie *The Pursuit of Happiness*.

> "Don't ever let someone tell you that you can't do something. Not even me. You got a dream, you gotta protect it. When people can't do something themselves, they wanna tell you that you can't do it. You want something, go get it. Period."
>
> -Will Smith
>
> (The Pursuit of Happiness, Film)

3. BE PREPARED

During her husband's presidential campaign, at the beginning of her speech, Michelle would sometimes make off-the-cuff comments that the opposition later used against her. Over time, she learnt how to speak her truth with the least possible amount of backlash. I say *possible*, because some of the attacks she faced were purely racist, without any reasonable basis. Until America gets to a better place, those are inevitable.

Like I said in the previous sections, we all need to put ourselves in positions where, when the opportunity comes knocking, we would be there to open the door. When you are always prepared, you become more confident to confront the unknown.

4. BELIEVE IN YOURSELF

Will Smith in an interview once said,

"Greatness is not some godlike feature that only a special few can achieve. It is something that truly exists in all of us. This is what I believe, and I'm willing to die for it."

He went on to quote Confucius;

"Those who believe they can, and those who believe they can't, are both usually right"

One of the ways to build your confidence is to believe that you can accomplish what you have set out to achieve. Not many successful people have special talents and not many successful people have special skill sets that make them stand out, but one thing is common among all these people. They had strong work ethics and believed that their hard work would pay off

5. NEVER FORGET YOUR PAST

Denzel Washington once said.

"Never forget where you came from because, at the end of the day, you are either someone or no one"

Remembering the true reality that you have chosen to move on from is a particularly useful way to build your confidence when making your choices. You get to a point of acceptance. You accept what happened in the past and understand why you choose to move on from it. When you are constantly reminded of how much you want to change your reality to a better one, you use the negative vibe as fuel to move you to want to build on that past reality as a steppingstone to your new reality. Now your past reality negative vibe is your reason why you are moving on for future possibilities of positive vibes which brings to light more confidence to face and take those calculated risks.

6. REFUSE TO SETTLE FOR LESS

"Small minds discuss other people, good minds discuss events, and great minds discuss ideas. There is no passion to be found in settling for a life that is less than the one you are capable of living"

-Denzel Washington

The decision to never settle for less is a significant confidence boost. It always keeps your hopes high and allows you to never belittle yourself or think little of how much you can achieve as a person. Like Michelle in the face of discouragement, refusing to lower her standard and choosing to apply to Princeton, when we all refuse to settle for less, we will always be confident enough to make choices that will be the best option to draw closer to the endgame.

Be like Marie, be like Lebron, be like Kevin, be like Michelle, be like Denzel, and be like Will! Take a step today towards an awesome tomorrow! With this book as a guide, march firmly into your new reality!

TAKE CHARGE!

19

Who Am I?

Thank you for getting this far! If you have read up to this point, chances are you might want to know who I am!

The name's Donell Edmond! Aka Danggit-Man (words from Joe king the Railroader). Am the Father of Kanden Edmond, son of Helen Edmond, a brother to the late Jamere Edmond- my childhood superhero, Jerome Edmond aka Romey B, Deles Edmond bka DilBeats, and Santacia Edmond childhood name Baby.

What type of person am I? Well, I wrote a poem to tell you just that; enjoy!

DEFINING ME

Humorous ... Knock Knock

Intelligent ... $E = MC^2$

Kind-hearted...Here is five bucks please eat

Gangsta ...Do things in life because I can

Caring ...If you like it, I love it

Good Guy ...Did you get the flowers I sent

Cool ...Yeah you see me checking you out

Positive...The sky might be the Limit, but our destination is the Stars

Loyal ...My name's not Waldo

Calm... like water on the feather of a Duck's back

*Understanding ...Sh*t happens, let's roll with it*

Passionate ... I am a lover, not a fighter

Confident ..."It's Freedom baby Yeah" "Oh behave"

Collective ...Only the beginning much more to come

Down to earth ...Accept life for what it is worth

Honest ...Yes, your booty looks big in those jeans

Spoiled ...You're overcooking my grits

Spontaneous ...Hey let's go to Disney World

Enlightening ...Grass is not always greener on the other side

Mama's boy ... My mama always said

Spiritual ...God walks with me

Sweet ...You look simply gorgeous

Good Listener ...Wow! your boss said what?

A gentleman...Here allow me to get that for you